Behind the Glamour

BEHIND [THE] SCENES
FASHION CAREERS

Susan Henneberg

Raintree is an imprint of Capstone Global Library Limited, a company incorporated in England and Wales having its registered office at 264 Banbury Road, Oxford, OX2 7DY – Registered company number: 6695582

www.raintree.co.uk
myorders@raintree.co.uk

Editor: Alison Deering
Designers: Heidi Thompson and Kayla Rossow
Picture research: Pam Mitsakos
Production specialist: Tori Abraham
Originated by Capstone Global Library Ltd
Printed and bound in India

ISBN 978 1 4747 3812 5 (hardback)
20 19 18 17 16
10 9 8 7 6 5 4 3 2 1

ISBN 978 1 4747 3815 6 (paperback)
21 20 19 18 17
10 9 8 7 6 5 4 3 2 1

British Library Cataloguing in Publication Data
A full catalogue record for this book is available from the British Library.

Acknowledgements
We would like to thank the following for permission to reproduce photographs: Alamy: Cliff Hide PR, 43 top right, Ovidiu Hrubaru, 40; Capstone Press: 44 top right; Getty Images: Beck Starr, 16 top right, BJI/Blue Jean Images, 22, Gabriel Olsen, 48 middle right, Hero Images, 12 top left, Jeffrey Mayer, 48 bottom right, Jordan Siemens, 53 middle left, Neil Mockford, 50 bottom left, Rolf Bruderer, 35 bottom right, Tasia Wells, 38 bottom middle; Newscom: Carlos Tischler/Splash News, 46 middle left; Shutterstock: Action Sports Photography, 33 top right, Africa Studio, 28 top, amixstudio, 25 bottom left, Andrey Armyagov, 33 top middle, Andrey_Popov, 24 top right, Andrii Kobryn, 17, Becky Starsmore, 19 top, Beer5020, 31 bottom middle, bikeriderlondon, 37, 39 top, 47, 56 bottom right, Blend Images, 12 bottom left, BlueSkyImage, 18 top right, BONNINSTUDIO, 9, 31 bottom right, Christophe Testi, 50 middle left, Comaniciu Dan, 14 top middle, Daniel Jedzura, 26 top right, Deborah Kolb, 49 bottom left, Deviant, 50 top middle, Diego Cervo, cover top left, 16 bottom right, Dikiiy, 44 bottom, Dmitry Kalinovsky, 60 middle left, Dragon Images, 24 middle, 43 bottom left, Eugenio Marongiu, 14 bottom left, 30 top left, fashionall, 38 top left, 38 top right, FashionStock.com, 4, 13, 18 middle left, 19 middle, 23 bottom right, 30 top right, Georgejmclittle, 55 bottom middle, Gina Smith, 57, goodluz, 58, GoodMood Photo, 55 bottom left, greenga, 14 middle left, 14 middle right, Iakov Filimonov, 36 middle right, 53 top left, 53 bottom left, Igor Bulgarin, 50 middle right, iofoto, 26 bottom right, Jaguar PS, 39 bottom, jgolby, 48 top left, Jordan Tan, 1, Karkas, 16 top, 33 middle, Kite_rin, 52, kubais, 18 bottom right, Lawrey, 27, lenetstan, 46 bottom right, leungchopan, 12 top right, lev radin, 61 bottom right, Liderina, 31 bottom left, MaleWitch, 10 left, meatbull, 23 bottom left, michaeljung, 54, Monkey Business Images, 6 top right, 34 top right, 42, 45 bottom right, 55 top left, Nejron Photo, 49 middle left, NemesisINC, cover bottom, Ollyy, 8, oneinchpunch, 61 middle right, Ovidiu Hrubaru, 28 bottom, 29 bottom, Pakawat Suwannaket, 33 bottom middle, Paul Matthew Photography, 46 bottom left, Pavel L Photo and Video, 21 bottom right, 26 top left, 51 bottom right, Pavel_dp, 20-21 top, Peter Bernik, 20 middle right, Photocrea, 24, bottom left, Photographee.eu, 7 top left, posteriori, 33 middle left, Preobrajenskiy, 38 bottom right, ProStockStudio, 60 middle right, racorn, 36 bottom left, Raisa Kanareva, 50 middle, Soloviova Liudmyla, 61 top left, SpeedKingz, 32, Syda Productions, 41 bottom left, Sylvie Bouchard, 11 top left, Tinxi, 10 bottom, Vagengeim, 7 top right, Vorobyeva, 6 bottom, Wallenrock, 21 bottom left, wavebreakmedia, cover top right, 6 top left, 15 top left, 29 top, 34 top left, 36 bottom right, 45 top right, 55 bottom right, 59, Yuganov Konstantin, 5, Yulia Reznikov, 30 bottom right; Thinkstock: gpointstudio, 38 middle left

Design Elements: Capstone Studio: Karon Dubke; Shutterstock: helen-light, Jozef Sowa, Le Panda, optimarc

Contents

"I DON'T DO FASHION. I AM FASHION."
– COCO CHANEL

Introduction

If you're like many young people, a career in the glamorous world of fashion sounds like a dream come true. Strutting down the runway in a stunning designer dress. Snapping photographs of famous models as they hit the catwalk. Scouring the trendy shops to style a celeb. The fashion industry can provide great career options for people who have a strong sense of style and love clothes. However, it can be competitive. Like you, thousands of other young people want to be a *Vogue* supermodel or a *Project Runway* winner. Only a handful make it to the top every year. The good news is the fashion world is huge and there are plenty of jobs to be found behind the glamour.

If you have a passion for fashion, then you have much in common with many of today's successful designers, photographers and stylists. While still teens, they sewed their own clothes. They devoured fashion magazines and blogs. They worked in retail. They worked hard to study fashion at college or university. There they learned about the wide range of occupations in the fashion industry.

You might be interested in the more creative side of the fashion world. If so, you can become a designer, photographer, display designer, make-up artist or stylist. Maybe you love to talk about fashion with your friends, which could lead to a career in fashion writing and public relations. Or perhaps you're fascinated by the business side of fashion. You might think about being part of buying, production and sales.

How do you choose which field is right for you? First things first – find out what you are passionate about. Earn a degree or diploma in a fashion-related field. Get experience as an intern or an assistant. Work hard, ask questions and take risks. There are huge opportunities in the fashion industry. It's a big, exciting world, just waiting for smart, creative, ambitious people like you!

CHAPTER 1

Display designer

As you walk by your favourite store, do the windows ever make you stop and take a second look? Do the displays make you want to rush inside and try on the clothes? If so, you have fallen for the magic of display designers and visual merchandisers. A display designer's job is to get you into the store. Once they've made a good first impression, they want you to stay and buy. How do they do that? It's all about telling the story.

Display designers pay close attention to what's going on in the fashion world. They have one eye on celebrity social media feeds and the other on fashion magazine spreads. They predict what shoppers will want to wear each season. And they make sure the store mannequins rock the latest trends. Display designers don't just want to sell you the top or the jeans or the cute jacket that pulls the look together – they want you to buy the whole outfit!

Visual displays reflect some kind of theme, such as springtime or an upcoming holiday. In large national chain stores, the head office assigns the themes. The branch stores then get detailed instructions on how to put together the displays. Designers often find creative ways to connect the clothes to your lifestyle. A mannequin wearing shorts, a crop top and carrying a tote full of accessories tells you it's time to get outfitted for a beach getaway.

Display designers also create displays for apparel companies at trade shows – large conventions with hundreds of booths. Each booth showcases products from different companies. At the annual New York Shoe Expo, for example, more than 300 footwear makers show off different brands of shoes. At trade shows, designers have more creative power – they come up with inventive themes and eye-catching arrangements to make their employers' goods stand out. Their job is to sell their clothing, shoe or accessory label to store buyers.

BOOTHS AT SI' SPOSAITALIA
EXHIBITION IN MILAN

So how can you break into this creative field? As with most careers in fashion, you need to be prepared to start as an intern or assistant to more experienced designers. A degree in art or fashion merchandising will give you an edge in getting hired and moving up. For now, get a head start by taking a closer look at the displays at your favourite shops. See if you can figure out what the display designers did to catch your eye. What story are they trying to tell?

At a glance

The basics: Display designer

Also known as: Fashion merchandiser

Overview: Display designers plan commercial displays to entice and appeal to customers. They change or rotate window displays, interior display areas or signage to reflect promotions or changes in inventory.

Education/skills required: Training in vocational schools, related on-the-job experience or a degree

Suggested courses: Art, interior design, stagecraft, business studies

Salary range: £19,750 – £74,300/year

Median salary: £21.20/hour or £44,140/year

FIRST PERSON: SHOPIFY

"Whether you're a small business retailer or planning your first pop-up store, your window display is one of the most powerful weapons... This is your chance to ... turn the heads of those passing by and engage them enough to stop, look back, and walk in to your store where your floor staff or products can sweep them off their feet and get them to make a purchase."

— Humayan Khan, visual merchandiser
at online shopping website Shopify

IT'S NOT ALL ABOUT STYLING AND PICKING CLOTHES. YOU HAVE TO BE HANDY. IN MY DEPARTMENT I'M WORKING WITH WINDOWS, AND WE HAVE TO CARRY MANNEQUINS UP LADDERS. WE HAVE TO BUILD, DRILL AND PAINT. IT'S A LITTLE CONSTRUCTION, A LITTLE ASSEMBLY, A LITTLE OF EVERYTHING.

— V ORPIANO, VISUAL MERCHANDISER AT H&M

CHAPTER 2

Fashion designer

Do you imagine seeing clothes you designed coming down the runway during Fashion Week? Or picture your shoes and accessories gracing the pages of your favourite magazine? If so, fashion design might be the career for you. Fashion design is one of the most glamorous careers in the fashion industry. It's also competitive. But don't let that discourage you. Fashion is a huge industry, and designers are needed in all different areas, including footwear, accessories, jewellery, wedding gowns and dozens of others.

Fashion design begins with a vision and a sketchbook. Designers do their homework before starting to sketch. They learn trends and find out what their customers want. They visit trade shows to find out what sells. Then they give their detailed sketches to the production team, which creates samples to show buyers.

Most new designers work for large companies – stores such as Gap, Marks and Spencer or Asda.

In these mass-production businesses, hundreds of designs are produced quickly, marketed and sold. Most of the time the design house's name is on the label rather than the designer's. Some designers hope to move up into ready-to-wear clothing for stores such as Harvey Nichols or Selfridges. There, designs will be more exclusive and promoted to upmarket customers. Others hope to get into couture, where one-of-a-kind designs are made.

"I FEEL LIKE AS A DESIGNER, YOU NEED TO BE ABLE TO COMMUNICATE AND WORK WITH PEOPLE. YOU DON'T HAVE TO BE AN EXPERT IN ALL AREAS, BUT YOU HAVE TO KNOW HOW TO DO ALL OF THEM. IF I HAD SOME FINANCIAL EDUCATION OR BASICS ABOUT A BUSINESS, THAT WOULD HAVE BEEN REALLY HELPFUL.

– REBECCA MINKOFF, FASHION DESIGNER"

If you're a budding designer, consider attending an art or fashion school. There you can build a fashion background and develop your skills. Work experience and internships are also a great way to gain practical experience and valuable networking contacts. Designers new to the field usually start as assistants before developing their own lines. Those who are creative and original can find a rewarding career turning their visions into reality.

At a glance

The basics: Fashion designer

Overview: Fashion designers create original clothing, accessories, and footwear. They sketch designs, select fabrics and patterns, and give instructions on how to produce the products they design.

Education requirements: Undergraduate degree in art or fashion design

Suggested courses: Art, clothing design and sewing, computer-assisted design (CAD), drawing and painting, textiles, business studies

Salary range: £26,650 – £100,670/year

Median salary: £24.60/hr or £51,170/year

FIRST PERSON: BIKINI PRODIGY

What's it like to become a fashion sensation while still in secondary school? "Bikini Prodigy" Courtney Allegra turned her dreams of becoming a fashion designer into reality before she was 18 years old. Called "fun and flirty," Allegra's line of swimsuits has been featured in *Seventeen* magazine as well as on the *TODAY* show and *Pretty Little Liars*.

"As far as swimwear goes, I inspired myself to start designing simply because I couldn't find the "perfect bikini," Allegra told *SuperFab* magazine in 2015. Next for her is a new line of men's swimwear.

> THE MOST IMPORTANT THING YOUNG DESIGNERS CAN DO IS BECOME AWARE OF THE WORLD AROUND THEM. THEY SHOULD BE INSPIRED BY THEIR ENVIRONMENT AND IMMERSE THEMSELVES IN CULTURE. TRAVEL; GO TO MUSEUMS; SEE FASHION EXHIBITIONS; STUDY FILM, COSTUMES AND MUSIC – EVERY ASPECT OF THE WORLD SHOULD SERVE AS INSPIRATION AND SPARK CREATIVITY.
>
> – MARY STEPHENS, DIRECTOR OF FASHION DESIGN AT FIDM

CHAPTER 3
Fashion make-up artist

If you've ever spent hours in front of the mirror carefully applying make-up, you know the skill required. Make-up artists can change an everyday look into anything from red-carpet glam to street-style punk. They are an essential part of any fashion team. No model would appear on the runway or in a magazine photo shoot without carefully designed make-up to complete the look.

A day in the life of a make-up artist is never boring – largely because it's never the same. As a make-up artist working in the fashion industry, you might spend a morning making up models for a local magazine fashion spread. In the afternoon you may be working on location for a TV advert. In the evening, you could be working backstage at a runway show.

While these changing jobs make the life of a make-up artist fun and exciting, they also make it challenging. Most make-up artists do not have permanent jobs. Instead they work as freelancers, and freelance work can be unreliable. Finding steady clients isn't easy. Smart make-up artists develop relationships with modelling agency managers and fashion photographers to find and create new opportunities.

Make-up artists are in especially high demand during major fashion weeks. Lead make-up artists meet with fashion designers and stylists ahead of runway shows in order to develop themes and looks. They apply make-up on a demo model for the rest of the artists to copy. Fashion week make-up artists learn to apply make-up quickly and accurately despite the stress and hectic pace fashion week brings.

ALL ABOUT MICHELLE PHAN

It's hard to believe that make-up mogul Michelle Phan was once rejected for a job at a make-up counter in a department store. Instead she began filming herself applying such looks as Snow White, Lady Gaga and geisha. By 2016 more than eight million subscribers were regularly tuning into her YouTube channel for make-up tutorials. Her popularity created opportunities for Phan. She created a make-up line called *em* and a beauty subscription service called *ipsy*. She films her videos, and the videos of the dozens of YouTube stars she mentors, in her own Southern California studio. Her biggest accomplishment? Allowing her mother to retire.

There are many ways to prepare for the fast-paced, creative career of a fashion make-up artist. Practise at home by following your favourite beauty vloggers. Work at a make-up counter to gain valuable experience. Attend beauty school to learn the basics of make-up. Even with practical skills and experience, be prepared to start as an assistant. With talent and hard work, you will soon be on your way to an exciting career as a fashion make-up artist.

At a glance

The basics: Fashion make-up artist

Overview: Make-up artists apply make-up for anyone appearing in front of a camera or live audience in film, television, theatre, concerts, photographic sessions or fashion shows.

Education/skills required: Beauty licence recommended

Suggested courses: Beauty, drama, film, photography, stagecraft, business studies

Salary range: £18,360 — £94,600/year

Median salary: £26.10/hour or £54,310/year

A DAY IN THE LIFE: MAKE-UP ARTIST CHARLOTTE TILBURY SHARES HER DAY

6.00 a.m. I sleep in my make-up. I'm never, ever seen without it.

6.30 a.m. I start to get dressed. I live in high heels — I've got maybe 300 pairs.

7.30 a.m. I have to be at a show at least two hours in advance. I bring six suitcases full of make-up — better safe than sorry.

1.30 p.m. At lunch I might discuss up-and-coming products, counter reviews, or marketing with my team. I basically have a mobile office.

4.30 p.m. I have to juggle meetings all the time. Today I have a meeting with an editor. We're launching my brand in Canada in June because the line is expanding quickly.

8.00 p.m. Finally I have time to relax with my friends.

1.30 a.m. I fall asleep quite easily because I'm exhausted. Live life to the fullest and make the most of yourself with make-up — that's my mantra.

"BEAUTY IS POWER, AND MAKE-UP IS SOMETHING THAT REALLY ENHANCES THAT; IT'S A WOMAN'S SECRET."

— CHARLOTTE TILBURY

CHAPTER 4

Fashion photographer

Photographer Mario Testino knows exactly when his star began to rise in the fashion world: "Gucci made the fashion world look at me. Diana made the whole world look at me," he says, referring to the day he photographed the glamorous British princess. While most fashion photographers don't have A-list clients such as Testino's, they can still earn a living doing the creative work they love.

Much like fashion make-up artists, fashion photographers typically work on a freelance basis. They may have an agent to help them find jobs and they network to find new clients. Ad agencies, shopping centres and catalogue companies all hire photographers to feature their products. One day a photographer may be shooting sunset photos of glamorous models. The next day, he or she might be in the studio for a catalogue shoot, photographing one pair of shoes after another, making each look on trend and unique.

TYPES OF FASHION PHOTOGRAPHY

Fashion photographs fall into three main categories: commercial, editorial and high fashion. Commercial images are all about selling the clothes. Outfits can be seen clearly and in detail. The models' make-up and hair tend to be simple so the clothes take centre stage. Editorial photographs are found in fashion magazines. They tell a story about the clothes in a series of shots on a specific location. For instance, the models wear dreamy, romantic clothing in an old castle or fun beach styles on a tropical island. In high-fashion photography, photographers shoot top models posing dramatically in a fantasy wardrobe. Open the next issue of your favourite fashion magazine and see if you can identify each category.

But there is more to being a successful fashion photographer than just shooting photos. Photographers spend as much time in front of their computers as they do their cameras. They download their photos. Then they sift through them, choosing the best. They use editing software to brighten shadows, correct the colour and change lighting effects.

As a fashion photographer, you'll also need to know how to manage your business. Photographers are responsible for keeping their own accounts, which includes invoicing clients and paying fashion teams and lighting technicians. Equipment costs must also be accounted for, and they can be extensive. Most fashion work is done with digital single lens reflex cameras. A camera for a beginner can

range from £2,000 to £7,000. Lenses, studio lights, computer hardware and software also add to the cost of doing business. A pro can easily spend over £25,000 on the high-quality equipment needed to produce images for magazines, billboards and websites.

CAMERA

LENS

At a glance

The basics: Fashion photographer

Overview: A fashion photographer takes pictures of people, landscapes, merchandise or other subjects, using digital or film cameras and equipment. He or she may develop negatives or use computer software to produce finished images and prints. Fashion photographers select the sites and backgrounds for photo shoots, help models pose to capture the best features of the designs and choose which photographs to feature.

Education/skills required: Training in vocational colleges, related on-the-job experience, or an art degree

Suggested courses: Art, film, photography, business

Salary range: £15,150 – £57,860/year

Median salary: £12.25/hour or £25,480/year

> 66 TAKE PICTURES ALL THE TIME. DON'T WORRY IF YOU TAKE A BAD PHOTOGRAPH: YOU LEARN MORE TAKING A BAD PICTURE THAN A GOOD ONE. IF YOU DON'T LIKE IT, STUDY IT AND FIGURE OUT WHY YOU DON'T LIKE IT. YOU'LL LEARN FROM YOUR MISTAKE.
>
> – PATRICK DEMARCHELIER, PHOTOGRAPHER 99

Fashion photographers get their start in a variety of ways. Some take a photography course at an art school. Others earn a degree in art at university. Almost all assist established photographers to learn the tricks of the trade and build their portfolios.

CREATING A PORTFOLIO

A portfolio of your best photos is the most important tool for a photographer trying to break into the fashion world. A website can showcase many photos for little money. However, most potential employers want to see what they call "your book." To make your book, print at least 20 good-quality photos measuring 10 x 12 centimetres. Have a variety of shots. You will want close-up portraits, groups of people and scenes. Above all, photo editors say, allow your personality to come through.

CHAPTER 5

Fashion writer

Do you love reading fashion magazines? Do you dream of seeing your writing in the pages of *Vogue, Marie Claire* or *Glamour*? With more than 200 different fashion magazines in print every month, that dream could become a reality. The fashion industry needs writers. The magazines you see gracing book shop shelves, magazine racks and newsagents are the oldest and most visible source of jobs, but there are many others. Trade journals such as *Drapers* and *Boutique* magazine hire writers to keep fashion insiders informed.

Print magazines aren't the only option for fashion writers, either. Most print magazines have websites that allow writers to post instant updates and breaking fashion news. Newspapers, reality shows and design house blogs also need writers and editors to create their fashion content. The most up-and-coming fashion writers run their own blogs. Some bloggers are even turning their passion for documenting their fashion lifestyles into full-time careers. Top bloggers can attract millions of followers to their websites. Thanks to their online presence, they're able to earn solid incomes from their websites, personal appearances and product endorsements.

STYLE ROOKIE

Tavi Gavinson was only 11 when she started her blog *Style Rookie*. In frequent posts, she showed off her quirky, unique style. The next thing she knew, she was sitting next to *Vogue* editor Anna Wintour at New York Fashion Week. She has been featured in *Teen Vogue* and starred in a video for fashion label Rodarte. Gavinson now edits an online magazine called *Rookie*. The site invites readers, including Sarah Silverman and Lena Dunham, to contribute writing, photography and other art. Gavinson's philosophy? "I think that fashion can be a tool of feminism and of self-expression and individuality and empowerment."

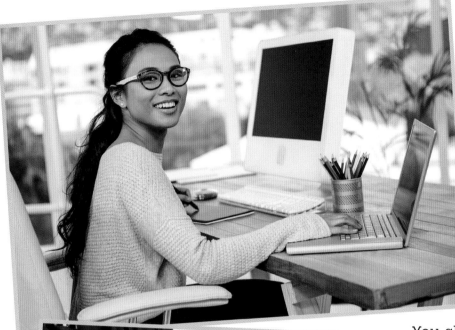

So how can you get started as a fashion writer? You'll need a degree to break into this field. Graduates with degrees in both journalism and fashion or a fashion-related field will have an edge.

You should also expect to work at least one internship as you get started. Most new writers start as interns and help their editors with many tasks. As you move up in the field, you'll have more input on what stories to include and which topics to focus on. Experienced fashion writers craft articles about fashion houses and explain new trends. They interview hot, up-and-coming designers. They also cover fashion shows and events. Keep in mind that even if a story doesn't seem groundbreaking, it's still important. New writers need to get clips – stories with your name as a byline.

VOGUE AS A TRENDSETTER

Most people working in fashion consider **Vogue** to be the most influential fashion magazine in the industry, if not the world. **Vogue** began in 1892 as a weekly newspaper for the elite of New York society and has been in print for more than 120 years. Publisher Condé Nast exported the magazine to Britain and the rest of Europe in the 1910s and 1920s. Now Anna Wintour, **Vogue**'s editor-in-chief, calls the magazine everyone's "glamorous girlfriend." Its September issues often exceed 600 pages.

At a glance

The basics: Fashion writer

Also known as: Fashion journalist

Overview: Fashion writers create features and copy for a variety of media outlets including fashion magazines, advertising and trade publications, newspapers, blogs and online magazines.

Education/skills required: Undergraduate degree in journalism, English, fashion design, fashion merchandising

Suggested courses: Media, English literature, journalism, public speaking

Salary range: £23,490 – £92,040/year

Median salary: £26.70/hour or £55,550/year

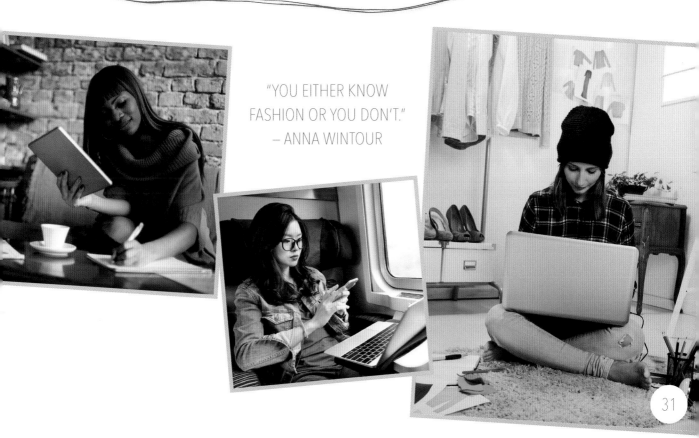

"YOU EITHER KNOW FASHION OR YOU DON'T."
– ANNA WINTOUR

CHAPTER 6

Retail buyer

Sure you love shopping – who doesn't? – but what is it like to actually buy clothes for a living? Retail buyers attend fashion shows. They travel the globe searching for new trends. They rub shoulders with famous designers. But being a retail buyer isn't all glamour. Making sure a store stocks items that will sell is a big responsibility. Buyers have to choose the right garments. They have to get the right sizes, quantities and prices. To do that, they need to know the customers they are buying for.

There are several kinds of retail buyers. Buyers for large, national chain stores such as Debenhams and Marks and Spencer specialize in one area. Some focus on dresses. Others handle sportswear or shoes. Buyers for fast-fashion stores such as H&M, Zara and Topshop, where new styles arrive weekly, have to stay on top of designer looks for their on-trend customers. Buyers in smaller independent stores need to be knowledgeable in all areas, from men's suits to children's clothes.

OPPORTUNITIES FOR TEENS: FASHION SUMMER PROGRAMMES

How would you like to get a head start on a career in fashion? Many fashion colleges open their doors during the summer to high school students. Nottingham Trent University and Condé Nast College of Fashion and Design both offer programmes for teens and have a wide variety of courses. You can learn about design, photography and writing. London College of Fashion offers programmes in fashion design, photography, styling and media. If you are in the United States, you can take classes in fashion design at the Parsons campus in New York. Parsons takes its summer class to Paris. If travelling to the major fashion hubs is out of the question, look closer to home. Just about every fashion or art school recruits teenagers for summer programmes.

Regardless of what type of store they work for, retail buyers all have two main goals. They need to buy goods that the store can sell at a profit, and they need to keep customers coming back for more. One of the most challenging parts of the job is predicting what customers will want. Buyers must work at least six months in advance. In order to predict trends, they read trade magazines and attend trade shows. They talk to designers and publicists. They meet with manufacturers. Good buyers keep an eye on celebrity trendsetters. They watch what is selling in other shops or websites and analyse what has sold in the past.

> " EARLY IN YOUR CAREER YOU MAY
> BE ASKED TO DO THINGS THAT YOU
> DON'T FEEL ARE WORTHY OF YOUR EDUCATION
> OR THAT DON'T SEEM EXPLICITLY RELATED TO YOUR
> CAREER GOALS. BUT IF YOU DO THEM WELL,
> THEY CAN INSPIRE PEOPLE TO PUT THEIR FAITH IN
> YOU AND GIVE YOU THE WORK YOU *DO* WANT.
>
> – AMY ASTLEY, EDITOR-IN-CHIEF
> AT *TEEN VOGUE* "

At a glance

The basics: Retail buyer

Overview: Fashion buyers purchase women's, men's, and children's clothing and accessories for both retail and wholesale stores.

Education/skills required: Undergraduate degree in buying and merchandising, general business, purchasing and contracts management

Suggested courses: Accounting, computer applications, business studies, marketing, principles of sales, retail marketing

Salary range: £24,271 – £76,830/year

Median salary: £20.45/hour or £42,550/year

So how can you get paid to shop for a living? There are lots of things you can do right now to increase your chances of getting hired as a retail buyer. If your school offers job shadowing or internships, see if you can arrange one with a local store buyer. Consider an after-school or summer job in a clothes shop to learn the business. When it comes time for university, take courses in fashion merchandising, business or finance. These degrees will give you an edge with hiring managers. With the right experience and education, you can turn your love for buying clothes into a fun and successful career.

A FASHIONABLE EDUCATION

Where's the best place to learn the ins and outs of the fashion industry? There are many top fashion schools in the United Kingdom. Central Saint Martins, Kingston University and the University of Westminster are all in London. There are also excellent courses at schools and colleges all over the country, including Nottingham Trent University in the Midlands and Glasgow School of Art in Scotland. There are also many prestigious fashion schools in the United States including Parsons School of Design, LIM, Fashion Institute of Technology (FIT), Pratt Institute in New York and the Fashion Institute of Design & Merchandising (FDIM) in California. There are good schools in other parts of the world as well. For international flair, consider Polimoda in Florence, Italy, or Bunka Fashion College in Tokyo. And don't rule out community colleges — many offer associate's degrees in apparel design or merchandising. Fashion experts emphasize that the particular school is not as important as the passion, energy and creativity that the graduates bring to a job.

CHAPTER 7

Stylist

Ever wondered how models in fashion magazines look totally chic and pulled together? Or how celebrities always seem perfectly styled on social media? What you are looking at is the work of fashion stylists. A stylist's job is to make his or her clients look their best. Many aspire to dress A-list clients with fashions from top designers. Styling is a fast-paced, exciting world, however, it's also a difficult field to break into. Fortunately, there are many opportunities to gain experience right in your own community.

A stylist's life is often a whirlwind of fashion-related activity. Attending trade shows and exhibitions, browsing fashion magazines and websites, keeping an eye on designer and celebrity social media feeds – all are necessary parts of the job. Creating and maintaining a client's personal style takes a talent for organization and attention to detail. As stylists create original looks for their clients, they also create their lookbook – a portfolio of photographs or magazine tear sheets in which their looks have been featured. A professional lookbook is a stylist's visual resumé.

> 66 THE TWO THINGS I REQUIRE BEFORE I WOULD EVEN MEET WITH SOMEONE IS AN ACTIVE SOCIAL MEDIA PRESENCE AND EXPERIENCE WORKING IN RETAIL. YOU HAVE TO BE INVOLVED IN RETAIL, IN MY OPINION, IN ORDER TO BE SUCCESSFUL.
> – NICK WOOSTER, MENSWEAR AUTHORITY AND J.C. PENNEY CREATIVE ADVISOR

"FASHION FADES, STYLE IS ETERNAL."
– YVES SAINT LAURENT

Fashion stylists are needed in a variety of places. You might work as a stylist or personal shopper in a store, putting together professional looks or perfect outfits for special occasions. You might be needed to create looks for catalogues or print ads. Photographers need stylists to dress models for photo shoots. Local news stations, wedding planners and ad agencies all need stylists to create unique style images.

ADVICE FROM A PRO

"Internships teach you how to start a job, how to finish the job, how to go from the show room to costume houses. When I was an intern for a stylist, I got to work with celebrities like Jeremy Piven and Christina Aguilera. From there, I started to put my lookbook together and was able to work my own jobs and get clients on my own, such as Selena Gomez... I would have never imagined there would be so much computer work. I'm researching different looks, making appointments, gathering all the pieces for a look. It's a lot of screen time!"

— Basia Richard, stylist to Selena Gomez, shares her tips for aspiring stylists

How can you land a job as a stylist? Most start as an assistant to a more established stylist. Or they intern as part of a fashion merchandising or fashion design degree. A background in fashion retailing can also help you get a foot in the door. Courses in business or accounting will be useful, as most fashion stylists are self-employed. If you want to work with celebrities, be prepared to relocate to the star capitals of the world – Los Angeles, California; New York City; London, England; or Paris, France. Wherever you land, spending your days making people look their best could be the perfect career for you.

66 AS A STYLIST, I UNDERSTAND HOW FASHION CAN AFFECT YOUR MOOD AND YOUR PERSPECTIVE. IT'S NOT JUST ABOUT THE CLOTHES. WHAT YOU WEAR IS A VISUAL EXTENSION OF YOUR SELF-EXPRESSION.
– RACHEL ZOE, CELEBRITY STYLIST 99

GETTING THE DETAILS RIGHT

"Even if you don't go to school for fashion, there are a few easy ways to learn about the details. Most people live near department stores, and if you're lucky, there's probably even a high-end boutique you can get to. Compare trousers and shirts you own to the pricier stuff, and really try to notice the differences in cuts and design. Turn those same garments inside out to see how they're made. Chop it up with different associates who seem to know the product, and learn what makes it 'good.' As you see more and more clothes from different designers you'll know your Balmain from your Balenciaga without having to look at the tags."

– Mathew Hensons, fashion editor for Complex Media, talks about designer clothes

At a glance

The basics: Stylist

Also known as: Photographic stylist, wardrobe stylist, fashion stylist

Overview: A stylist is a consultant who selects the clothing for published editorial features, print or television advertising campaigns, music videos, concert performances and any public appearances made by celebrities or other public figures.

Education/skills required: University degree in fashion design recommended

Suggested courses: Fashion design and/or merchandising, communications, marketing, art history or photography

Salary range: £27,360 – £63,860/year

Median salary: £39,590/year

66 IT'S IMPORTANT THAT YOU KNOW FABRIC, IT'S IMPORTANT THAT YOU KNOW TEARING AND PATTERN MAKING. IT'S REALLY VALUABLE, BECAUSE A LOT OF THE TIME YOU WILL END UP REDESIGNING OR CO-DESIGNING. MY CLIENTS ARE SO INCREDIBLY BEAUTIFUL, BUT THEY'RE USUALLY NOT 6'0 MODELS. THEY ARE ACTRESSES AND THEY HAVE PERSONALITY, SO FOR EACH ONE YOU KIND OF HAVE TO CUSTOM FIT THE GOWNS TO THEM.

– NICOLE CHAVEZ, CELEBRITY STYLIST, SPEAKING TO *EXCLUSIVELY FASHION* MAGAZINE 99

CHAPTER 8

Fashion marketing & public relations

Where do design, sales and journalism come together to form one amazing career? Fashion marketing and public relations (PR) professionals are found on the front lines of the fashion industry. If you are outgoing, creative and a strong communicator, fashion PR may be the perfect place for you.

As a PR specialist, your role is to act as the face of the fashion label you represent and work hard to make that brand successful. To do that, you need to get your products in front of customers. Successful PR specialists organize product launches. They plan fashion shows and in-store events. They ask designers to talk to the media. They interact with fashion editors to get their products in magazines and on websites and collaborate with stylists who use their product line.

ADVICE FOR ASPIRING PR PROFESSIONALS

"Learn as much as you can about the industry by taking advantage of all the great fashion industry publications available to you online. Start a blog; write about the brands you love. Grab friends and spend the weekend doing crazy photo shoots. Learn photography; learn to edit those photos. Take classes in coding and graphic design. Don't wait for permission — just start your own thing."

— Crosby Noricks, creator of online fashion
public relations site PR Couture

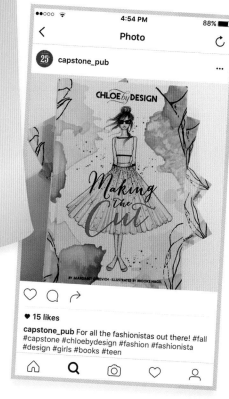

To make it as a marketing or public relations professional, you'll need top-notch communication skills. Publicists need to be confident speakers. They need to write clear, persuasive blog posts and press releases. You'll also need an active social media presence. An important part of a publicist's job is managing blogs and social media accounts. For many publicists, their brand's Instagram feed is as vital as its presence in *Vogue*.

So how can you get started now? Look for opportunities to speak and write about topics you're passionate about. Check out job shadowing or internships with a PR professional. Research colleges with courses focussed on fashion marketing and public relations. Follow your favourite clothing brands or designers on social media, and take note of the strategies they use to grab your attention. When the time comes to launch your career as a PR professional in the fashion industry, you'll be ready to jump in head first.

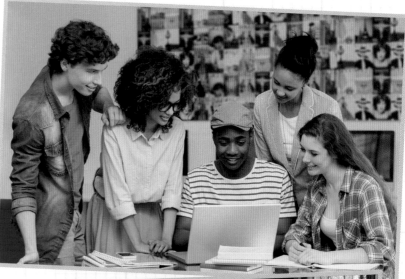

INTERNSHIPS: A FOOT IN THE DOOR

Whether it's at a store, a design studio or a fashion label, internships are especially vital in the fashion industry. Student interns often work for no pay, but they gain huge rewards in experience and valuable contacts. They get to network with industry professionals. Many interns also get

credit toward their degrees — they typically work several days each week, which allows them to attend classes the other days. If you're lucky and work hard, an internship could turn into an entry-level position after graduation.

At a glance

The basics: Fashion marketing specialist

Also known as: Public relations specialist, PR specialist

Overview: Marketing managers plan and execute the best ways to promote their employer's products, services or brands.

Education/skills required: Undergraduate degree in marketing or public relations

Suggested courses: Accounting, banking and finance, computer applications, economics, business studies, marketing, psychology, statistics

Salary range: £25,470 – £388,470/year

Median salary: £21.93/hour or £45,630/year

OUTDOOR
FASHION SHOW
PREPARATION

CHAPTER 9

Costume designer

Costume designers have one of the coolest jobs in the fashion industry. They create designs for theatre, dance, opera, circus, concerts, television, film and theme parks. Sometimes they translate comic book figures into film superheroes. Or they re-create the country life of 1920s British aristocracy. Cinderella, Big Bird and Beyoncé have all been transformed because of the work of a costume designer.

If you love history, literature, and theatre, costume design would be a great career for you. To accurately re-create the fashions of a historical period, you'd need to know all about the life and customs of the time – everything from clothing to shoes to accessories. You need to know how people dressed and how they styled their outfits to fit the time and their lifestyles.

COSTUME DESIGNERS GUILD AWARDS

On one special day each year, the Costume Designers Guild (CDG) rolls out the red carpet to celebrate artists' achievements. This association protects and improves the status of costume designers. The CDG gives awards to costume designers for motion pictures, television and commercials. Past winners in film include the costume designers for *Mad Max: Fury Road*, *Into the Woods* and *The Hunger Games: Catching Fire*. Television costume designers have won awards for *Game of Thrones*, *Downton Abbey* and *Glee*.

TRISH SUMMERVILLE, COSTUME DESIGNER FOR *THE HUNGER GAMES: CATCHING FIRE*

For some costumes, a knowledge of the human anatomy is essential. Costumes have to be fashioned so that performers can actively move, which may require you to use different kinds of materials. For instance, designers use a special fabric for superheroes so the performers don't get too hot. Other costumes require special fasteners so that performers can quickly get in and out of them. Collaboration skills are also essential – it's up to the costume designers and the director to create a shared vision of the characters, brought to life by the costumes.

66 WHAT A COSTUME DESIGNER DOES IS A CROSS BETWEEN MAGIC AND CAMOUFLAGE. WE CREATE THE ILLUSION OF CHANGING THE ACTORS INTO WHAT THEY ARE NOT. WE ASK THE PUBLIC TO BELIEVE THAT EVERY TIME THEY SEE A PERFORMER ON THE SCREEN HE'S BECOME A DIFFERENT PERSON.

– EDITH HEAD, LEGENDARY HOLLYWOOD COSTUME DESIGNER **99**

Ready to see if costume design is for you? Try your hand at creating unique costumes for yourself, your friends or your siblings. Volunteer with the costume department at a local theatre.

Investigate costume design programmes at art schools, colleges or universities. During or after studying, an internship or apprenticeship will help you gain experience and create valuable networking contacts.

DESIGNING REY'S COSTUME FOR
STAR WARS: THE FORCE AWAKENS

After reading the script for **Star Wars: The Force Awakens,** costume designer Michael Kaplan knew the kind of costume that the character Rey needed. She was poor and worked as a scavenger. The planet was a hot desert. So Kaplan designed versatile dust-coloured garments made out of natural materials. The criss-crossed gauze top could be used as a rope or pulled up to keep sand out of her eyes. The tunic could keep her warm or be wrapped around her head to keep her hair out of her face. Rey's goggles, if you look closely, appear to be made out of old Stormtrooper headgear. The earth colour identified her as part of the Rebel force. A flowing scarf, signifying the exciting movements to come, flaps behind her in the first scene. Every detail in Rey's costume tells the story of this exciting new character.

REY'S WAX STATUE AT MADAME TUSSAUDS

At a glance

The basics: Costume designer

Also known as: Costume attendant

At a glance: Costume designers are responsible for the overall look of the clothes and costumes in live performance, film or television productions.

Education/skills required: Undergraduate degree in fashion design or fashion merchandising

Suggested courses: Art, clothing design and sewing, computer-assisted design (CAD), drawing and painting, textiles, history, literature, business studies

Salary range: £15,720 – £73,490/year

Median salary: £17.20/hour or £35,760/year

Be prepared for some challenges with this career. Costume design work can be seasonal. Jobs may only last a few weeks or months. You may have to move to a large city to find TV, film or theatre work. But if the idea of transforming a person into a character in a whole different world is irresistible to you, then costume design may be a perfect career.

CHAPTER 10

Boutique owner

Are you a determined shopper looking to express your own unique sense of style? If so, you have probably discovered the magic of boutiques. These stores truly reflect the individuality of their owners. The word *boutique* is French for *shop*, however, it was in swinging 1960s London, not Paris, that boutiques earned their mod reputation. They fed a new desire for clothes that were fun, affordable and unique.

Owning a boutique allows you to combine a love a fashion with a desire to be an entrepreneur, but it's also a lot of work and a significant time commitment. Opening and running a successful boutique requires you to be a jack-of-all-trades. A successful owner knows how to do everything from arranging displays to keeping the books. He or she also attends trade shows to purchase inventory.

A successful boutique owner is likely a people person. To keep the store up and running you'll need some important people skills, such as managing your employees, motivating them to do their best, and resolving any conflicts that arise. You'll also need to know your customers – especially what they can and will buy. For instance, you may want to attract young adult workers who need professional clothes. You may focus on a small area, such as high-fashion shoes or handmade jewellery.

There's more to owning a boutique than just shopping and knowing trends. As a boutique owner, you'll also need a background in business. You will be actively involved in ordering inventory, keeping the books, paying your employees and managing the store. You may need to get a loan from a bank to start the boutique.

> 66 IF YOU EVER THOUGHT OF OWNING YOUR OWN BOUTIQUE, IT WOULD HELP TO KNOW HOW TO RUN A STORE FIRST. WORKING FOR A CORPORATE CHAIN OR FRANCHISE NOT ONLY GIVES YOU THE EXPERIENCE OF RUNNING A SHOP, IT ALSO HELPS YOU DEVELOP A BIRD'S-EYE-VIEW OF HOW THE INDUSTRY OPERATES.
>
> — JIAN DELEON, FORMER EDITOR AT COMPLEX MEDIA 99

FAST FASHION

If you are like many young people, you love to shop at stores such as H&M and Zara. The clothes are trendy and inexpensive. But are they environmentally friendly? Some fashion critics call these clothes "fast fashion." Fast fashion clothes follow new fads, but fads change quickly. Clothes end up only being worn for a short time before being discarded — many end up in landfills. Critics recommend consumers recycle the clothes — or better yet, avoid fast fashion altogether. Instead of following the latest trends, buy well-made clothes designed to last. Set your own trend of thinking about the environment instead of the latest new top or skirt.

More and more boutique owners are using the internet and social media to gain customers. You may decide to have an online presence. That way you can make sales to customers outside your area. Your boutique may be entirely online, eliminating the need to pay for a physical space other than a warehouse for storing the inventory. However, you will need to buy and learn to use online tools, such as creating and maintaining a website, taking payment and shipping sold items.

At a glance

The basics: Boutique owner

Also known as: Entrepreneur

At a glance: Boutique owners purchase inventory, hire and manage employees, keep the accounts, negotiate property leases, and market and sell merchandise.

Education/skills required: University degree in business or accounting recommended

Suggested courses: Accounting, banking and finance, computer applications, economics, introduction to business, marketing, statistics

Salary range: £16,070 – £104,480/year

Median salary: £39,730/year

Boutique owners don't necessarily need a degree, however, courses in fashion, accounting and business are useful. If you think being a boutique owner would be the perfect career, try getting a job in one first. This would be a great way to get work experience. You can find out if owning a boutique is the right career for you.

STARTING AN ONLINE VINTAGE BOUTIQUE

These days anyone can become a boutique owner. The Internet makes it easy for fashionistas with a little money and a lot of ambition and time. All it takes is an account with an online marketplace such as Etsy or eBay. Here are the steps to creating an online vintage shop.

1. **Find your inventory** – This means going to second-hand shops, charity shops and car-boot sales. Look for pieces that are in good condition. On Etsy, vintage means at least 20 years old.

2. **Set prices** – Compare your items to other items online to set a fair price. It helps if you can put a date on an item. Look in old online catalogues for a match to your pieces. Customers may pay more for authentic clothing from the 1950s or 1960s.

3. **Take detailed photographs** – Use a model or a mannequin so customers can see how it looks on. If you use a model, don't show his or her face, to protect privacy.

4. **List measurements, not sizes** – Sizing has changed over the years. You don't want your customers unhappy because the clothes don't fit.

5. **Use social media** – Social media apps are a great place to advertise your items. Starting a blog can also help customers find you.

6. **Ship the clothes** – As soon as the order comes in, get your clothes packed up and sent to buyers ASAP. Keep on looking for new items to sell.

CHAPTER 11

Get ready for your future!

The fashion world is a huge industry with many options for careers behind the glitz and glamour of the runway or camera. But how do you know which direction to take when planning your career? Think about how you would answer these questions.

1. What are your best subjects in school?
   - Art: Consider display, costume design or photography.
   - English: Think about a career in fashion writing.
   - Maths: The business side of fashion might be for you.

2. What are your personality strengths?
   - I'm confident and outgoing.
     - Consider marketing and public relations.
   - I'm creative and adventurous.
     - Look at being a make-up artist or designer.
   - I'm focussed and well organized.
     - Buying or production might be your area.

3. What is your fashion style?
   - I love to rock second-hand shop finds!
     - You might love creating a unique boutique.
   - I sew my own unique designs.
     - You are on your way to a career as a fashion designer.
   - I shop my way to the latest trends.
     - You would make a great stylist!

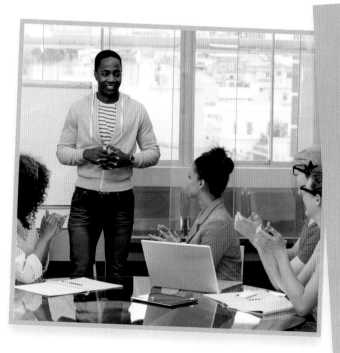

WHEN YOU SEE AN IMAGE THAT YOU LOVE, RIP IT OUT AND SAVE IT FOR REFERENCE. MAGAZINE COVERS, PICTURES OF PAINTINGS, ADVERTISEMENTS, ANYTHING – COLLECT THEM ALL. WHETHER YOU WANT TO BE A DESIGNER, A STYLIST, A FASHION EDITOR, A MAKE-UP ARTIST OR A PHOTOGRAPHER, THESE IMAGES WILL SERVE AS INSPIRATION TO YOU AS YOUR CAREER PROGRESSES.

– GLORIA BAUME, FORMER FASHION DIRECTOR AT *TEEN VOGUE*

Ten tips to get that future started!

1. Learn to sew your own clothes.
2. Work hard in maths lessons. You will need it when taking measurements or keeping the books at your own boutique.
3. Work at a retail clothing store to learn about clothes and customers.
4. Save money for university or art school.
5. Ask for art, photography and fashion books for your birthday.
6. Make a fashion lookbook of your favourite designs torn from magazines.
7. Practise photographing your friends in their most creative looks.
8. Create a fashion blog or vlog.
9. Start a fashion club at your school.
10. Practise applying make-up on your friends.

It's easy to dream of being a glamorous supermodel, posing in front of the camera. But the careers behind the camera can be just as exciting. The challenge is to learn as much as you can about them. Find your passion. Nurture your talents and acquire the skills you need. Be ready to work hard and start at the bottom. Mentors in the industry have all been there and are willing to help. Take their advice, and you too can make your dream of a career in fashion come true.

"AROUND SIXTH GRADE, MY MOM AND I FINALLY FOUND A PAIR OF MEN'S JEANS THAT FIT ME WELL. IT WAS AN AMAZING MOMENT TO GO TO SCHOOL WEARING JEANS LIKE MY FRIENDS. EVERYONE WAS COMMENTING ON HOW COOL THEY WERE. THAT'S THE MOMENT I MADE THE CONNECTION BETWEEN FASHION AND SELF-ESTEEM. I BECAME REALLY ADDICTED TO THAT FEELING."

– AIMEE CHESHIRE,
FOUND OF ONLINE SHOP
HEY, GORGEOUS!

" I FEEL THAT A LOT OF THE TIME PEOPLE ONLY SEE THE GLAMOROUS SIDE OF IT. AND THAT'S A GREAT PART OF IT. BUT THAT'S ONLY ABOUT TWO PER CENT OF IT, AND THERE ARE SO MANY PEOPLE WORKING SO HARD. I REALLY ADMIRE THE PEOPLE WHO WORK FOR ME THAT I CAN TELL CARE JUST AS MUCH EVEN THOUGH THEY DON'T HAVE TO. THOSE ARE THE PEOPLE THAT GO ON TO DO BIG THINGS.

– REBECCA MINKOFF,
FASHION DESIGNER

REBECCAMINKOFF

FIND OUT MORE

A Teen Guide to Eco-Fashion, Liz Gogerly (Raintree, 2013)

Fashion Photographer (The Coolest Jobs on the Planet), Justin Dallas and Rebecca Rissman (Raintree, 2015)

Fixing Fashion: Rethinking the Way We Make, Market, and Buy Our Clothes, Michael Lavergne (New Society Publishers, 2015)

WEBSITES

www.arts.ac.uk/fashion/

Learn more about the London College of Fashion and studying towards a career in the industry.

www.britishfashioncouncil.com/Education/BFC-Colleges-Council/ Member-Colleges

Learn more about the British Fashion Council.

www.fashionunited.uk/

Get up to speed with what's happening in the UK fashion industry right now.

ABOUT THE AUTHOR

Susan Henneberg is the author of numerous non-fiction books for children, teens and young adults. As a high school teacher and college instructor for over 30 years, she specializes in books that help students think about careers. She lives and works in Reno, Nevada, United States.

WANT TO LEARN MORE ABOUT
THE CAREERS BEHIND THE SCENES
IN SOME OF THE WORLD'S MOST
GLAMOROUS INDUSTRIES?

CHECK OUT THESE TITLES TO GO
Behind the Glamour
IN MUSIC AND FILMS.